invisibles Two

HIDDEN PICTURE PUZZLES

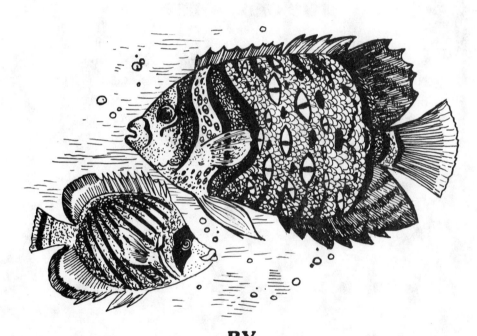

BY

Larry Evans

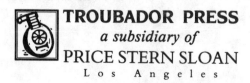

TROUBADOR PRESS
a subsidiary of
PRICE STERN SLOAN
Los Angeles

IN VISIBLE 1

THE OLD HOUSE

The ancient Victorian house has been visited by at least five brave (and foolish) children during the past 20 years. None of these children have ever been seen again.

How many lost children can you find?

P.S. Don't you dare go inside.

15 14 13 12 11 10   ISBN: 0-8431-1711-7

IN VISIBLE 2

SUMMER VISIT

Mary Ann is spending the summer with her Aunt Sophie. She is having a good time, but she misses her cat, Mehitabel and her dog, Wiener.

Please help Mary Ann find her pets.

IN VISIBLE 3

THE OLD NORTH BRIDGE

The battle of Concord was the beginning of the end of British authority in the American Colonies. Here at the Old North Bridge the Minutemen routed the Redcoats and paved the way for the second Continental Congress. The history lesson now being over, see if you can find George Washington, his wife, Martha, and good ol' Ben Franklin.

IN VISIBLE 4

KING WILLIAM'S SHIP

In 1066, William, Duke of Normandy, assembled a great fleet to invade England. His goal was to overthrow Harold and become the King of England.

The problem is: William the Conqueror cannot be found on his ship.

Can you find King William (wearing his crown) so he can lead his troops on to England?

INVISIBLES 5 · 6 · 7 · 8 · 9 · 10

THE SLEEPING PRINCE

Once upon a time, there was a magical kingdom, ruled by a wise and noble king. The king's only son was handsome, bold and did everything right.

A beautiful princess lived in the neighboring kingdom. She spent her days within a lush garden, surrounded by her five handmaidens.

One spring day, Elizabeth, the princess's favorite handmaiden, rushed into the garden. She was breathless, as though she had run a long way, and the tale she told filled the princess with dread.

"My lady," she said, "today, while the handsome prince was sleeping in his garden, a wicked old witch cast an evil spell upon him."

HIDDEN ARE: The king, the king's horse, the king's sword and the king's jester.

"And, my princess," Elizabeth went on, "suddenly the prince was no longer a handsome lad, but instead, a green and horrid frog."

Just then, the Lord Mayor's son, Howard, entered the garden. He had plucked a lily from the river's edge to give to the princess. "He did it," cried the handmaiden, "Howard paid the wicked old witch to cast a spell on the prince."

**HIDDEN ARE: Two frogs, the wicked old witch
and the beautiful princess.**

Now Howard was also a handsome lad and his love for the princess was known throughout the land.

"'Tis not true, my lady, that I paid the wicked old witch to cast a spell on the prince. I spent my last ducat on this giant lily so that you would know of my love for you."

The princess held out her hand to Howard, but she was unsure of his real feelings. After all, she had seen that very lily growing beside the river.

HIDDEN ARE: The king, a frog, the prince and the wicked witch's gnome.

The princess gathered her five handmaidens together and requested that Howard leave the garden. She summoned her father, the Hooded Knight, to protect her. Her father, in turn, summoned his wizard who rode in on his magic camel.

The wizard told the princess that if she would kiss the first frog she saw, her prince would return and all would be well in the land.

The princess was at first overjoyed at the wizard's spell. But, alas, she could not find even one frog in her garden.

HIDDEN ARE: The Hooded Knight saluting his daughter, the wizard, his camel and the fifth handmaiden.

Suddenly, right before the princess's eyes, a frog appeared. She quickly kissed the frog, but it just hopped away.

From the far corner of the garden came waves of laughter. "Ha ha," said the prince, "the trick's on you — I never really was a frog. It all was just a joke."

That night, the prince played his harp and entertained the court. The princess, having no sense of humor, married Howard and moved to Scotland where they opened a restaurant. The specialty of the house is FROG'S LEGS.

P.S. The prince and Elizabeth got married and had 10 children. The first word each child said upon reaching the age of one, was — RIBBITT.

HIDDEN ARE: The witch, the wizard and a frog.

HIDDEN ARE: The Hooded Knight, the wizard, the witch, a frog and a sword used to prepare frog's legs.

IN VISIBLE 11

DOWN BY THE OLD MILL STREAM

The two fishermen are spending the day across from Toll Gate number three. They have no idea that they are accompanied by fish, horses, goats, elephants, people, frogs, cows and an enormous variety of other animals.

See how many hidden people and animals you can find.

IN VISIBLE 12

THE OLD SWIMMING HOLE

Four boys are playing hooky on a warm spring day. They think they have fooled everyone. Mr. Smith, the truant officer, is about to fool them. He has hidden their clothes. It may be a cold walk home.

Find Mr. Smith, a shirt, a tennis shoe, and a pair of pants.

IN VISIBLE 13

THE PIRATE

Mr. Blackbeard is proud of his booty of gold and jewels. He doesn't realize that his cook (the one with the peg leg) has stolen a dory (a small boat) and escaped with the crown jewels.

Find the ship's cook in his stocking cap, a cannon, the dory and the peg leg.

IN VISIBLE 14

THE DONKEY'S SECRET

Farmer Brown's farm has chickens, goats, cows, pigs and, of course, a donkey and bunny. The donkey is the only animal that knows there are *other* secret animals hidden on the farm. Since he is going to tell Mr. Bunny, he might as well tell you.

See if you can find the secret animals.

P.S. They are a lot older than you think.

IN VISIBLE 15

JACK AND THE GIANT

Simple Jack has sold the cow, planted the magic beans, climbed the beanstalk and met the giant. Now, with your help, he must find the golden goose, the cow and his mother before escaping.

IN VISIBLE 16

THE GIANT
AND JACK

Now that you've found all the objects hidden in In visible 15, help the giant find Jack. After all, what's fair's fair.

IN VISIBLE 17

THE INDIAN SCOUT

H. P. Finder is the famous Indian scout. This doesn't mean that he is an Indian — it means he's *looking* for Indians.

Help ol' H.P. find an arrow, a bow, an Indian brave and a teepee.

IN VISIBLE 18

THE TROLL'S FOREST

Charlie has fallen off the trail for the third time. His dad wonders why because Charlie is usually a good hiker. What they don't know is the forest that they are hiking in belongs to four trolls. Next time, they plan to push Charlie and his dad into Bottomless Canyon.

Can you find the four trolls in time?

IN VISIBLE 19

THE CANDYMAKER

Little Henry Green has been sent to the market to buy some fruit and vegetables for supper. His mission may be in doubt though, as he pauses in front of the candymaker's shop.

Help save Henry from a spanking by finding the fruit and vegetables in the picture.

HIDDEN ARE: An apple, a slice of watermelon, a bunch of grapes, a pear, peas in a pod, a carrot, a banana and an ear of corn.

IN VISIBLE 20

THE HIDDEN FOREST

The peace of the forest has been broken by someone who has chopped down a tree. He may be one of those people from In visible puzzle number three. Find the famous tree chopper, his axe, a bear cub, a toad, a raccoon, a skunk, a chipmunk and another deer. Once you do, peace will return to the forest.

P.S. Tilt the page up close to your eyes to find the wood chopper.

SOLUTIONS

1

2

3

4

5

6

7

8

9

SOLUTIONS

10

11　**NOTE: This picture was taken from a postcard dated 1888.**

12

13

14

15

16

17

18

SOLUTIONS

19

20

FRONT COVER

BACK COVER

Two more hidden picture books
from Troubador Press

Troubador Press books are available everywhere books are sold,
or may be ordered directly from the publisher.

TROUBADOR PRESS

a subsidiary of

PRICE STERN SLOAN